The
Creative
Awakening

This is an illustrated journey which will assist you
in your spiritual awakening in this new Aquarian Age.

The
Creative
Awakening

WILL STEPHEN

"A Fool Fantasizing His Existence At The Expense Of His Destiny"

BALBOA.
PRESS
A DIVISION OF HAY HOUSE

Balboa Press books may be ordered through booksellers or by contacting:

Balboa Press
A Division of Hay House
1663 Liberty Drive
Bloomington, IN 47403
www.balboapress.com
1-(877) 407-4847

Because of the dynamic nature of the Internet, any web addresses or
links contained in this book may have changed since publication and
may no longer be valid. The views expressed in this work are solely those
of the author and do not necessarily reflect the views of the publisher,
and the publisher hereby disclaims any responsibility for them.

The author of this book does not dispense medical advice or prescribe the use
of any technique as a form of treatment for physical, emotional, or medical
problems without the advice of a physician, either directly or indirectly. The
intent of the author is only to offer information of a general nature to help
you in your quest for emotional and spiritual well-being. In the event you use
any of the information in this book for yourself, which is your constitutional
right, the author and the publisher assume no responsibility for your actions.

Certain stock imagery © Thinkstock.
Any people depicted in stock imagery provided by Thinkstock are
models, and such images are being used for illustrative purposes only.

ISBN: 978-1-4525-4626-1 (e)
ISBN: 978-1-4525-4627-8 (sc)
ISBN: 978-1-4525-4625-4 (hc)

Library of Congress Control Number: 2012901083

Printed in the United States of America

Balboa Press rev. date: 4/10/2012

CONTENTS

SELF PORTRAIT OF WILL

PREFACE

The spirited person has soul, where the conformist person has ego. Soul seeks real and true, while the ego accepts pretend and the socially acceptable way of thinking as a life style. The spiritual is accurate, while the conformed is full of illusions, lies, and deception. The spiritual you can feel. The conformed you must think. The spiritual person is individualized while the ego tripper must have the approval of others.

This conflict is at the basis of all persons embarking on the creative life. To be? or not to be? Will you allow your own unfolding for yourself? Or will you accept the advice of others as your guide?

To the artist the most challenging way is always the lure of the unknown. The easy way is always lacking and without imagination and is in a constant state of redundancy. Where the creative way is thrilling and different every time, while doing your creative life you're in the zone, and the zone is in constant change.

PART I

CHAPTER 1

"Where Do the Creative Come From?"

Creativity in it's basic form, is a "primoral reaction" associated with the "flight response" of the "instinctive response system" which is used for emergency escape or near death survival situations. This response to extreme or threatening danger, is brought out in modern man by "child abuse," psychological abuse, accidents, head traumas, and near death experiences. This is not to say that people with none of these extremes have no creativity. It merely implies that the greatest extreme at the earliest age is the force that has the most significance on the personality of the creative child, and the earlier, the better.

The desperation caused by abuse is so repulsive to the soul that the soul protects itself in flight, or flights of fantasy, or flights of inventive creativity. These turmoil's caused by abuse and inconsiderate treatment, are the volcanoes of creativity waiting to erupt in all great artists. At last they are able to express the tempest in their tea pot of volatile emotions on canvas with paint or music, song or survival, with design. When we respond creatively to need the psychological pattern is complete. Production usually becomes a proportion equivalent to the amount of pain endured by the sensitivity of the artist. When we respond with desire our hopes neutralize the natural response. The artist does not create from want. The artist creates from a need to create. To allow that need to unfold is the flowering of your self expression. Without it, you are only typical. But, with it, you are exceptional. The unfolding is central to an individuals' realization of self knowing. This self knowing allows the real you, to really, express the real you. The hesitant, "thinking," self, and the self that believes that their apprehensions are true. The left brain analysis won't work with the feeling soul. The left brain shines in the halls of civilization and it's precepts of control over the individual. The rules are a trap to the creative thinker. Redundancy is boring. It must be different every time for the quick witted artist, whose, "reality", exists in the spontaneity of the "creative impulse." ...And not in the planned agenda of regimented learning of the conformed, but, "reasonable mind set," of the socially acceptable way of thinking.

The creative mind is exceptional by comparison to the typical mind set of the narrow minded conservative thinker and non-creative person.

This conflict of the spontaneous creative and the narrow minded rule follower is the creative person's dilemma. To be narrow, "want" security and creature comfort over freedom of mind and uninhibited access to primoral instinctive skills, only available to non-conformed primoral woman.

SCANDINAVIAN GIRL

CHAPTER 2

What Makes Creativity Work?

The first ingredient is the discontented child, who is in conflict with his surroundings. He develops imaginative escape scenarios to withdraw into for emotional protection from a threatening or hostile world.

The second ingredient, is the realization you like your make believe world better. Then the greater the pain the deeper into the imagination you get to go, and the more elaborate the lure of the scenario that keeps you from having to face the scene back in the black and white world of the typical family. The artist can get lost in his own scenario of himself. But, this is only for the developmental learning part, of the imagination and evolvement.

Like any other tool the imagination gets more skilled with use, just like art itself.

The imagination and focus of concentration of the artist started as an escapist tendency and developed into a capacity to envision great and complicated systems, with interrelating operations, and patterns capable of coming together into magnificent accomplishments, like: amazing stories, movies, paintings, concepts, and other notions of reality.

For the conservative narrow mind of "the typical," all rules enforced, all people must do the same thing; think the same; agree on what is right and wrong; and never be mean, and always be nice.

The non-conformist artist on the other hand strives for the new; the unknown; that which has never been seen before; the wonder of your own uniqueness. An artist knows everyone has a completely different story. No one is the same. Everyone has a different color coded package of emotions of varying intensities, directing their perceptions and the expression, of everything they see. Nothing is static in a creative mind. The whole thing is in constant change.

The growth, and the absorption of ever more input multiplying into even more data, until it becomes impossible to remember, and this realization causes you to forget everything. At this point you must let go and let God. You must stop your attempt at controlling the destiny that God has planned for you. You must allow the unfolding of your reality. The assumption that "you know," has put dents on all our heads. Mother Nature knows what she made you for, and you must comply or die to your destiny. Die to the social order or die to your spiritual life. You are either spirit or *you* are physical.

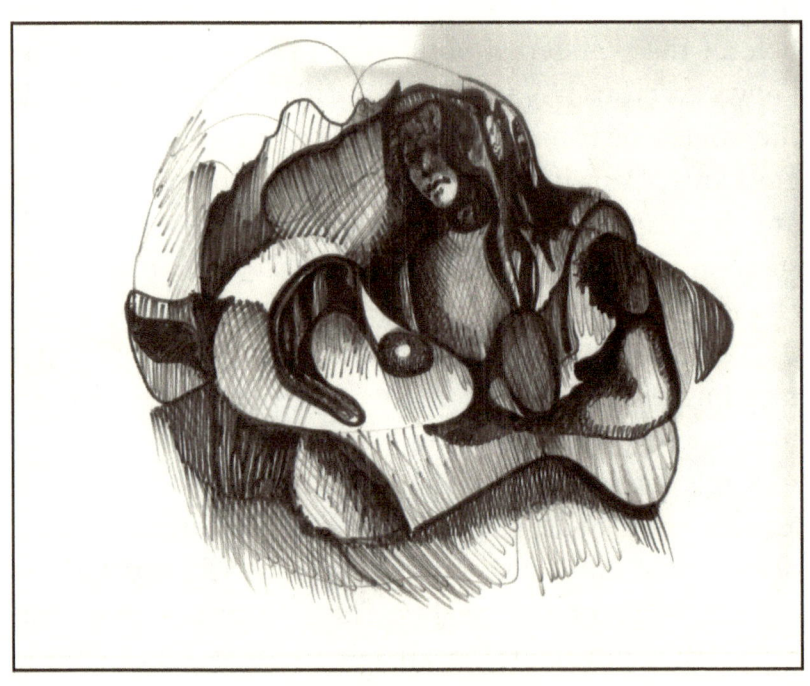

PRAYER CIRCLE

CHAPTER 3
The Purpose

The direction the energy of creativity comes from is love. The need to express love is the artist's gift. Love is like light; it brightens everything and makes it right. Just loving is reward in itself. That's why it's so important what you do with it. Loving the negative makes you smaller. Loving the positive makes you grow. But, loving what you do is the most important, because that is what "you" do, to express yourself and what you think and feel. This is who you are under the mask you wear for others. In the fabric of the universe, everything is accounted for.

There is purpose and meaning in everything, as long as your mind remains open. When it slams shut, you can no longer see, what you saw, before you slammed it shut. So, keeping an open positive mind is very important and necessary for a mellow, happy life's trip.

The purpose for this is to express what one experiences. When the mind closes itself around rules of conduct, moral training, redundant educational techniques and the laws of conformity and proper conduct, it ceases to operate independently.

The spontaneous creative reaction is stifled completely. "The memories of what went before," dominate the solutions of the mind and the creative source is lost. However, we have the natural laws of the creative mind, vs. the civilized laws of man. The purpose is to find yourself, ...within the nature of things.

Finding a place in society doesn't count. Our purpose is to define "the real self," that lies under the conditioning of our parents, schooling, and other social conformities, and learn to think for ourselves. The independent creative mind, "is," the spiritual trip. It's the soul trip. Finding the essence of a perfect life, is what we should seek and making our world perfect, one individual at a time, should be our life's goal.

GEMINI

CHAPTER 4
The Foundation

The foundation of the basic structure is a four side foundation. The foundation in the creative mind is the color spectrum from the sun; red, yellow, and blue. These primary elements are further broken down by blending the right and Ief1 colors, once for the three primary colors for a secondary level. Then doing the same thing again with the six secondary colors and finally ending with a twelve color spectrum. Now where the four sided foundation has four alternate points of view, the imaginative way has twelve and each is different by their own personal color code, allowing you to absorb much more data than the normal humanoid.

Twelve times at first observation, but, it quickly metabolizes in a chrysalis of input in the imagination. Meaning, the idea spreads to equal your imagination in your mind.

One might say the colors from the sun are the inspiration of the creative artist in the colors he/she might use to express herself, (the right brain). The conservatives think black and white and the creative feel in color. Black and white is the structure of what is, and color is the entire imaginative possibilities one could add to make the black and white world not so drab, and to add the rest of the dimensions under the sun. Women are the chosen; her mind abounds in colorful feelings.

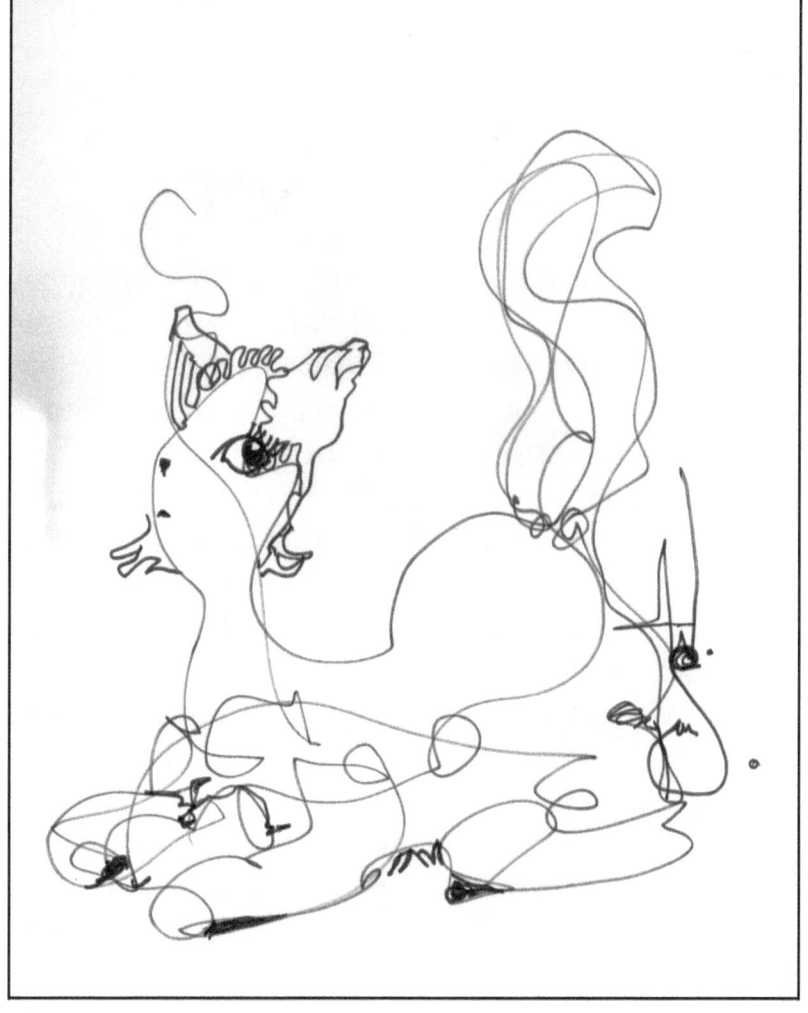

DELIA

CHAPTER 5

The Expansion

With use, the extra sensory facilities will grow, without use they will shrink. Consequently, the civilized wish it to cease and the spiritual wish it to grow. A one way point of view of the black and white mind is not a match for the wit and the open passions of the soul.

The simple conclusions of a "goat herder" cannot compare to a Michelangelo conceiving a Sistine chapel in the Vatican. However, Michelangelo was once on the same level, before he allowed the unfolding of his creative soul and the star within to shine.

The complexities everyone else saw were to him no more than watching his own "personal goat herd." As simple as looking into the palm of his hand , and that wouldn't be complicated at all except for all those lines. The concept of expansion couldn't be addressed without realizing the purpose you could fulfill if your body were functioning perfectly.

To have perfect health ...for the mind, body, and the soul. The mind and body should dance to the song of the soul. One should note here the over achievement of modern times destroys the "art of the "physique," and the perfecting of oneself. The fluid well danced and well tanned body is a breath taking thing to behold. These perfectly expressed bodies are not won by aerobic jumping, and backwoods jogging of the prize fighter. But, the fluid arts of flowing veils of a dance with grace and a stretchingly dynamic line, done to the rhythm of the harp (guitar) flute and drum, accompanied by a song of soulful content.

As a sanctuary ...from the rat race, of "the human dependents." Those pretenders who divert the heart of the sensitive artist, and cause the delay that frustrates the artist, and has ill effects on the artists primary life. You 'got' to 'be you' to 'be you'. No gettin' around that. When you don't know what that is, you must run everywhere looking, like the mad hatter in Alice in Wonderland." I'm late; I'm late, for a very important date. Oh, my! Oh my! Where am I going?" Slowing down is one attitude away. Doing it right is the next.

LEO RIZING

CHAPTER 6
Doing It Right

Everybody can do it but, nobody gets it right. ... Everybody is looking for "something better," when nobody is doing it "right." Doing it right is more concerned with simplifying procedures and dissolving inhibitions and road blocks to the free flow of self expression that makes up the creative life. The ability to do everything from the tips of your toes to the end of your out stretched fingers in both your mind and your body is the out reaching expression of the soul. To reach delirious expression of theta in all the arts is the dwelling of Venus. Venus is the patron God of the arts, love, and creative expression. Doing it right means: to seek your highest potential, while you withdraw into your own ship and start steering yourself. Be the captain of your own ship. Remember your rank.

You never stop directing your own movie. And, ...only when you get a bit part in somebody else's movie. It's hard to figure what to do, when your head no longer works. Then, you must do it with your heart. Your heart, will tell you what's best for you. When that's all done, "there is but to do it." You must go, by what you feel. What do you "need" to do? The "need," is the "motivation" that leads to "inspiration," and onto "creation."

Doing it right is directly connected to feeling good ... about you. Never lie, cheat, or steal. It, leads to distrust of others. Seek the truth and realize the truth is also, the best "possible" way. Satisfaction guaranteed.

WISHFUL THINKING

CHAPTER 7

Expanding, "By Doing It Right!"

"You" get everything with yes, and nothing with "no."

"No," ceases expansion. When you say yes, you open access to your imagination, and can overcome any inhibiting idea. Thereby overcoming it's negative effect on "your" imagination," and/or your creative self expression. Which means your imagination is your most creative tool. It's also at the foundation of your ability to grow and succeed in a financial way. It takes no imagination to survive by having a job. You must apply your imagination to interpersonal relationships. Unfortunately, this dissipates your creative abilities 100%. It's one or the other, making it a lifestyle change, rather than a part time hobby.

Stepping through the looking glass to the interior you, with it's depth and talent takes great courage, and is not for the meek. Only the bold would go, where angels fear to tread. This mental state is the land of the free and home to the brave.

The open mind is reward in itself. In it all decisions are left up to the fates and your agility at your self expression sets you aside from the typical, and sends you to the land of the few and you learn to accept your own "exceptionalness" and allow the fates to show you; your own unfolding.

While you laughingly, learn to express your love. Love is what grows; hate is what ceases love and growth. Expansion is the purpose of the universe, and light is the means of expansion, and satisfaction is the reward.

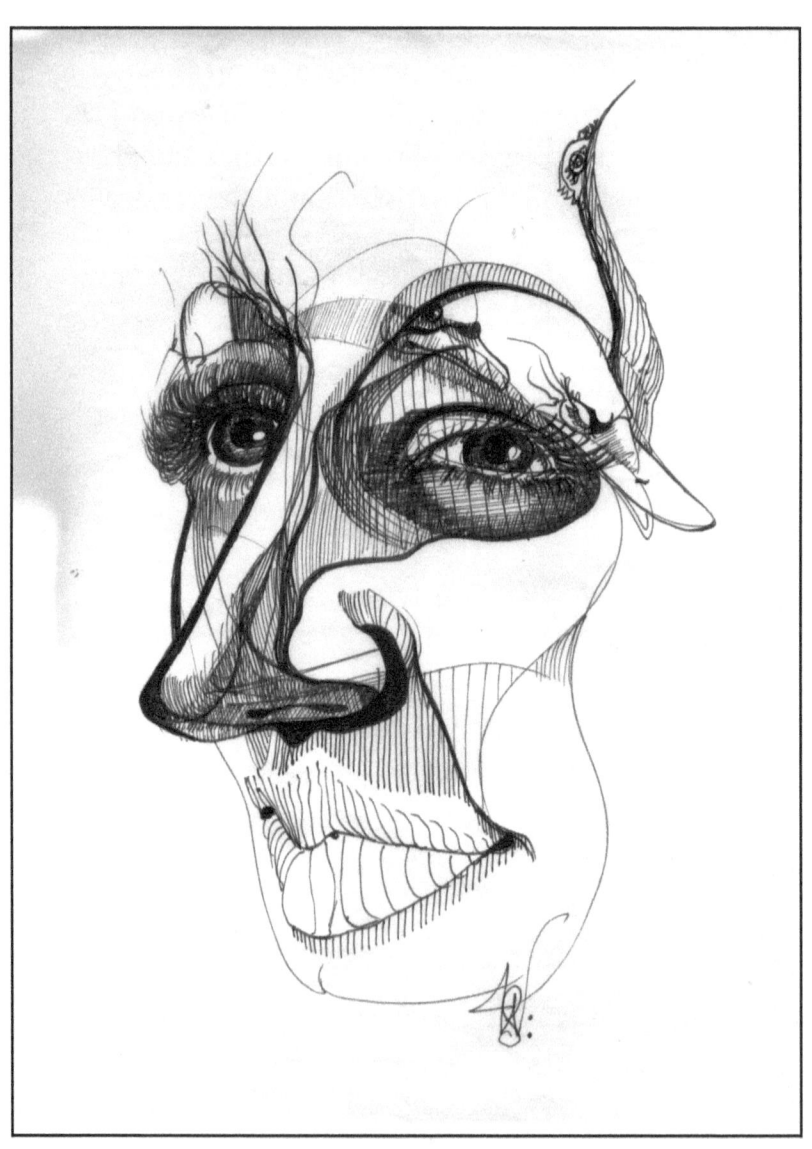

ROMAN THINKER

CHAPTER 8
The Spiritual

The spiritual, the sensual, the creative, the flexible, the natural, and love, are all the same concept. The function is the same. The words used to describe the events are different, allowing for their different origins. Each suggests another type of expansion, or better yet, "unfolding." It all comes from within. That which comes "from outside is probably tainted with conformity, and a non-creative response. A perception that is more ego oriented than spiritually oriented. Seeing, through the point of view of the socially acceptable way of seeing, is a far cry from seeing it in *your* own unique and individual way. To be who you are you must give up wnat other people think, and follow your own feelings about it, not other peoples feelings, but, "your" feelings. ...Your real feelings. Those feelings you hide from others, for fear of criticism or reproach. These ideas or feelings "are" who you really are.

The nice you, is the 'you', you wear a mask to conceal, the way you really feel, from your friends. These people of course are merely your social friends , (those people you use to find Mr. Right, or a job, or a discount, or one of a million other reasons people get together in a superficial way) in an attempt to fill the void in their soul with large numbers of superficial "friends." Rather than a few good friends, they can share their life with. ...Those who you can be yourself with, and will accept you as you are, and for whom you are. Real is always the best way. It all boils down to quantity verses quality. If, you always buy first class, you won't need to replace your needs, so often. This idea extended for a life time is a considerable savings.

Expression is the gift from the Gods. It. allows you to know yourself, know others, get smart, play music, take photographs, play guitar, paint pictures, dance expressively and grow to the point where you can allow the genius in you to surface and the true thing that God, made in you, to open, as a flower in spring.

CROWDED ROOM

CHAPTER 9

The Realization

The realization that, there is more to be known, than, "just the obvious." There are many levels of perception with every possible level of insight. The deeper you go, the less like the surface it seems. One begins to see the wisdom of the fool, which suggests the world is backward from any approach that would lead to a happy ending. And, which, for the most part is also philosophically true.

The unique number of variables in the perceived world is too great to be able to mentally cope with. The result is that our only hope is in our ability to retain an "open mind," by realizing anything is possible at any time, and you must be prepared to perceive it. It maybe complicated, so, don't be thinking about parties, ball games and social status. Put those aside, and think about what's really important.

In the end, you realize that, you can't really fight, what is supposed to be. When you do, you lose. When you go along with the program everything works out perfect.

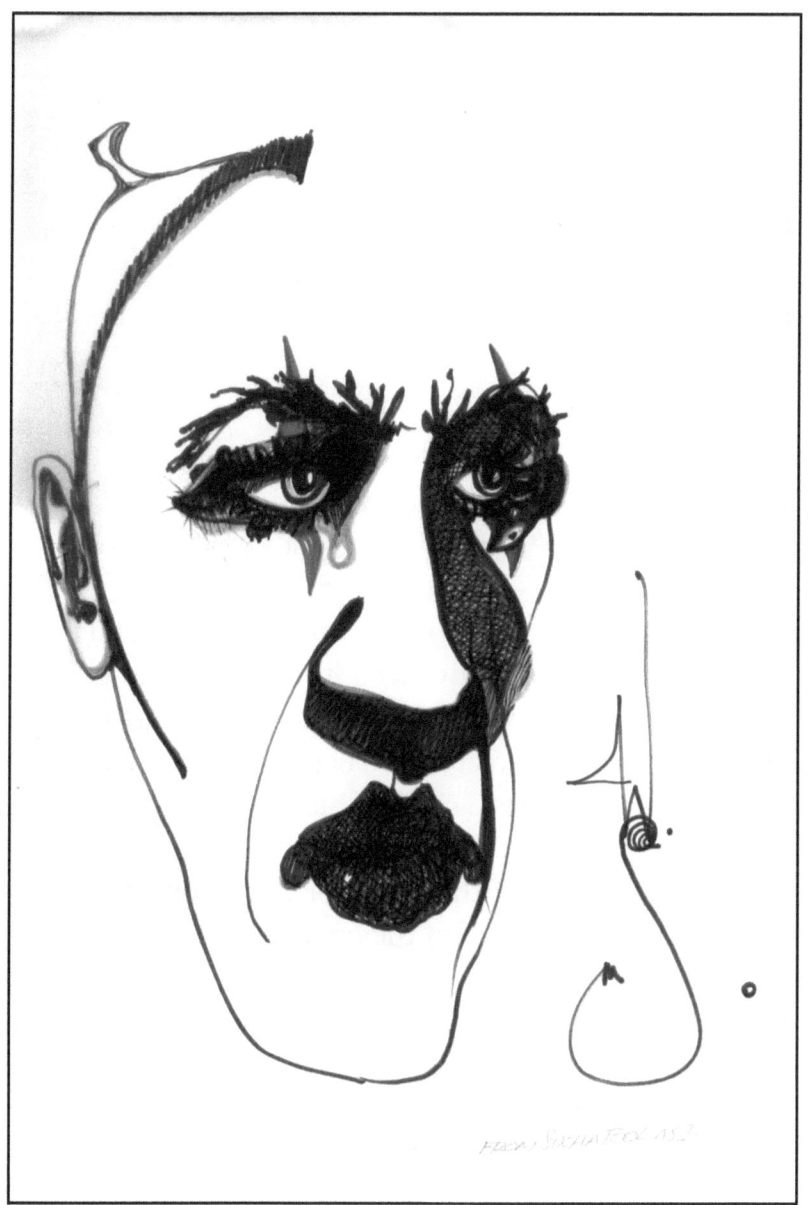

THE FOOL

CHAPTER 10
The Practical

What works, is practical. What works perfectly, works perfectly. Practical is the first step to perfect. The thing must "work," to have a practical value. With the creative it is always "need" that motivates the natural urges to create. In the more advanced it is the need to express some great love or pain. The foundation for great art is either great pain or great love. These passions are the raw material for the artist to nurture his/her needs to express. The expression itself comes from two separate places. The surface personality of the body; or the "physical world" view, on one hand, and on the opposite side of the teeter tauter is the Spiritual self or the soul. If, you use your head and the civilized approach, you must conform to the status quo, or the socially acceptable way of thinking. This is why we have a left brain. It's a very practical approach to solving problems; (on the physical plane of existence) this is all well and good for the person who expects a typical life: (the many).

For the deeper level individuals, those who have transcended the body, we find the artist who seeks to express the soul. The spiritual life is exposed to us, once we leave the narrow minded, superficial socializing, that leads to reproduction of children, and the continuance of the reproductive family way of survival, (the many). When we turn our backs on these values and demand that we express our very soul; the essence of our being when we do anything, ...then we are in the zone, and we are expressing what we were created to create in our quest to expand onto the universe with light.

We are either a body trying to survive and reproduce, or we are a soul, trapped in a body, that must transcend that body, in order to express itself. We either see our lives as a primitive, purposeless reproducer, here only to ensure the survival of the species, or we are the entities that lurk in the deeper part of our mind and soul. That entity which is not limited by the body's insensitivities, and can realize what the truth is, by how your heart responds to it. The purpose for your deepest part is the expression of art, beauty, and the perfecting of your surroundings. You are a reproductive monkey or a creative soul. That seems like a practical solution to me!

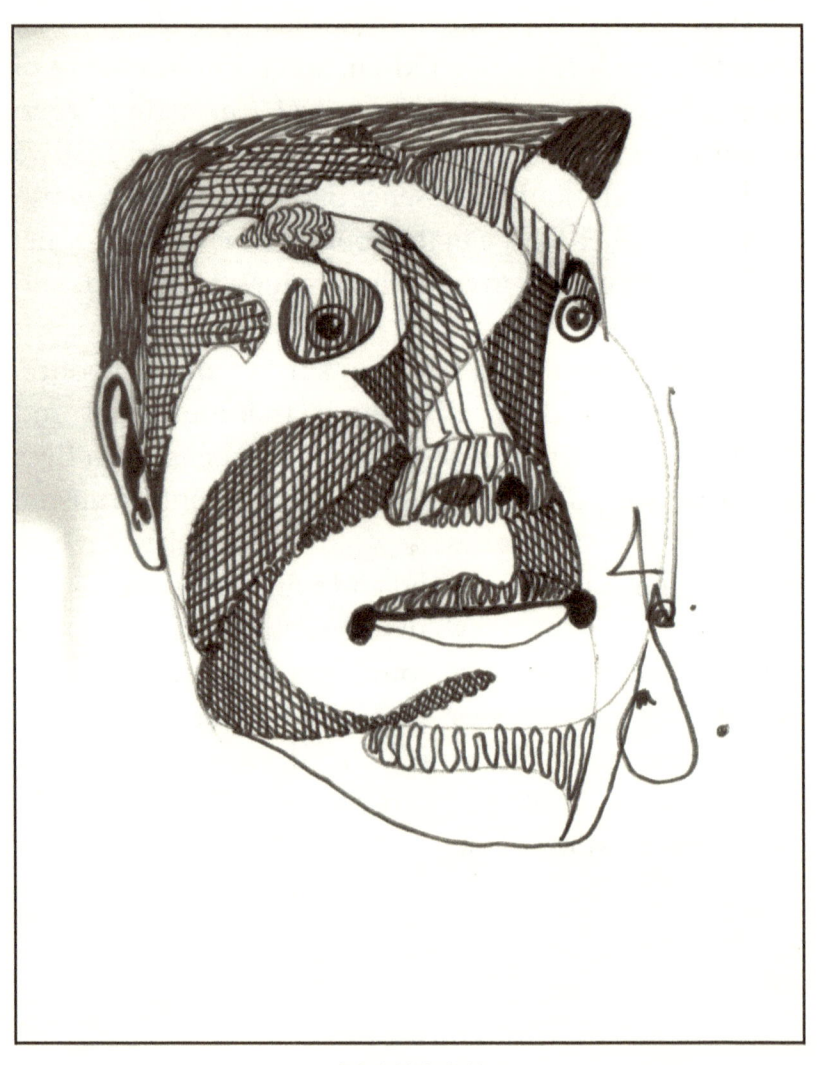

BRANDON

CHAPTER 11

The Out Flowing

The creative achieve satisfaction by expressing their deeper feelings and inner most workings, as a guideline for the less sensitive or less intuitive creatures that also inhabit our space.

Love is the only thing you can give away and still have more to give, as it is the only thing that grows with giving it away. Memory is our library of reserve defenses. It works when you tell a child "not" to play in the street. Memory is to the left brain rule orientation. Creativity is to the heart's soulful expression. When you give of your left brain, you give the rules of conduct. The right brain is feelings of the body. Emotions and passions are the expression of the soul. The soul is the deepest level that can be reached in a body. There are other levels, but, the body must be transcended first. Once done, the soul is at liberty to express itself. The method of expression is revealed by the passion you have for the things you love the most. These are the things that expose your soul to you. This out flowing is done by the sun for her planet type eggs; for a mother bear and her cub; a human mother and her baby; or a queen bee to her hive.

Life itself is an out flowing of light, disguised as nurturing. With the creative, that out flowing is expressed in music, song, dance, guitar, painting, any of the personally expressive route to the perfect destiny. One could truly say, "in God's world, you get what you give. Not what you want, but what you need.

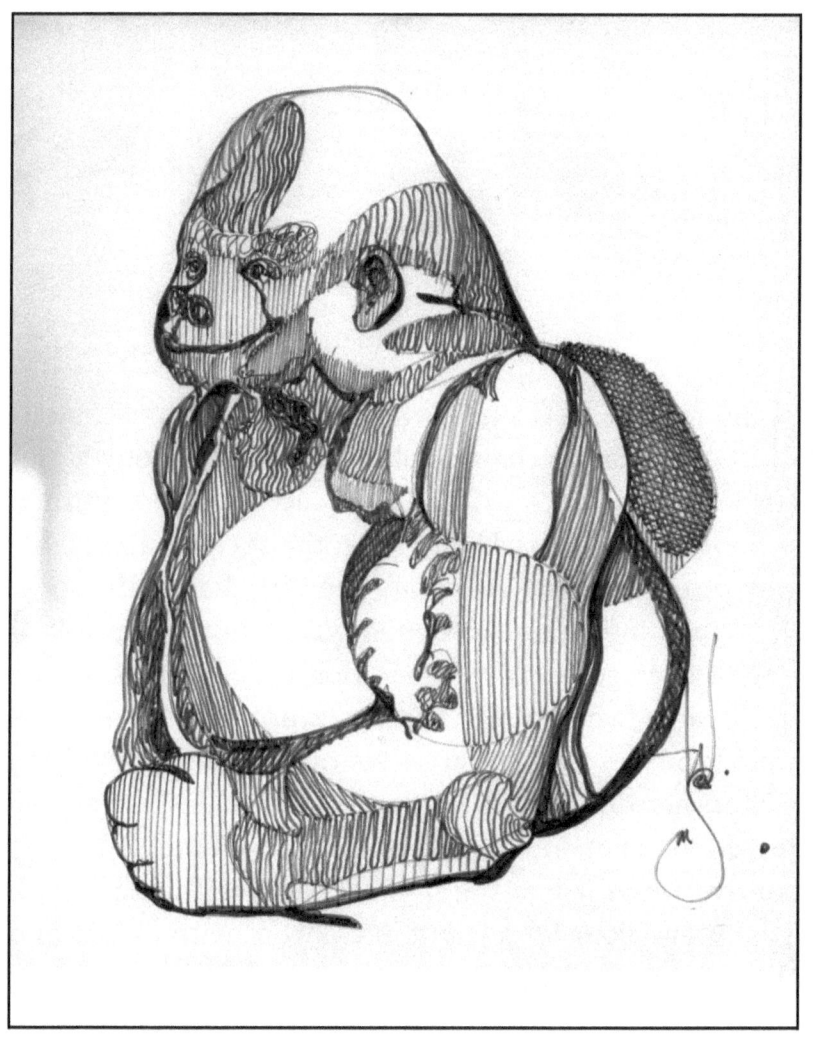

JOURNEY BY CO-OPERATION

CHAPTER 12

The Final Stage

The resulting effects of the first eleven transitions is the realization that the philosophy of the court jester (that world is backward, and to be successful in anything, is merely to do it backward from the socially acceptable way of thinking.) Nature has been in charge all along. We (mankind) have never had one minute's control, of any of our ego stroking plans that never worked in the first place. Even though we never noticed, because we were too busy patting ourselves on the back and telling each other how smart we are. While we destroy all the life giving elements in nature that allows our species to survive when it hits the fan, everyone will be affected. That is everyone who is not in Concord with nature and the spiritual and a creative way of survival. Be what God made in you.

Don't listen to those who don't see your beauty. They don't love "you," any way. They love what they get from you. But, that is not good enough. When someone really loves you, they love you if you're crippled or not. When you love someone you over look their scars and pain and seek their light that you might blend /our light and become whole. "God is good."

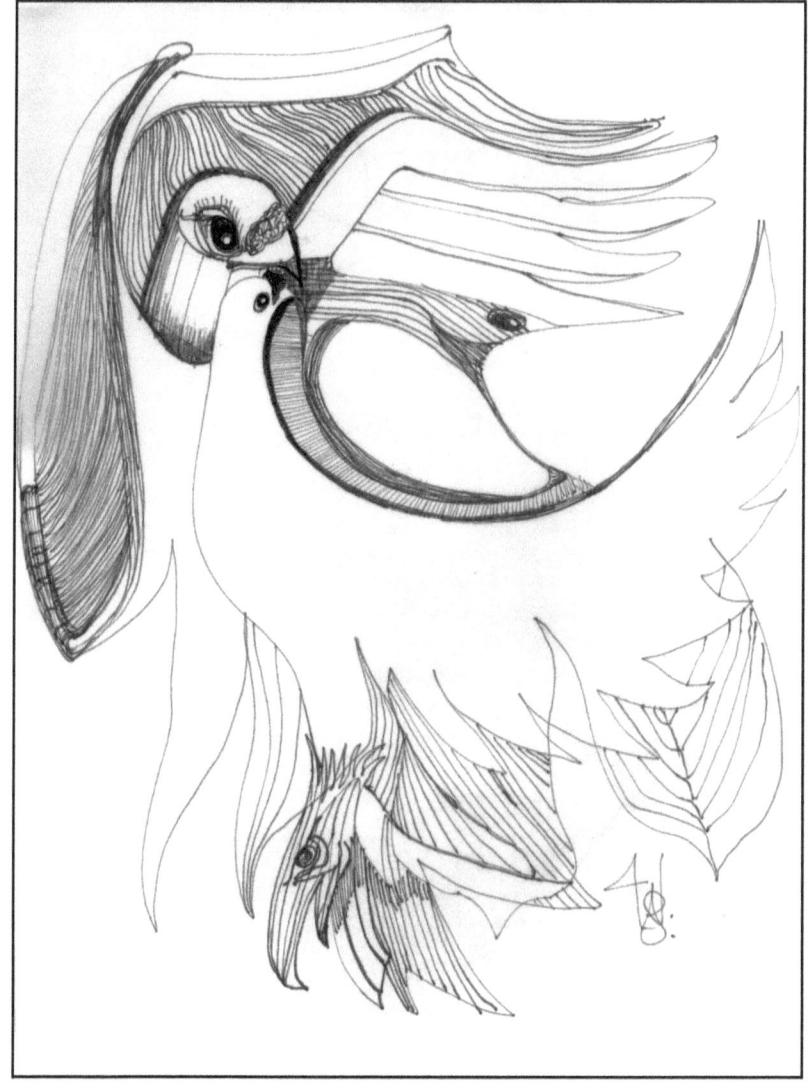

SOUL MATES

PART II
"THE CONCEPTS OF CONCORD"

PREFACE

When I was fourteen, I had an appendectomy. During which I was legally dead for twenty minutes. These twenty minutes have become the most important single event in my life, other than birth. While I was dead, I went into the light. There I was met by a man, a woman, and another man, who stayed at a distance. The man said to me, "You can stay if you want, or, you could go back and help make Concord. I hesitated and I was back to Earth and my material plane existence.

From this experience I have measured my whole life in an attempt to understand what He was talking about! I had heard the word referring to Concord, Massachusetts and some vague battle or some other revolutionary war event. Other than that, I had no idea what it meant. I spent the next forty-six years of my life trying to find out what it meant and what it was my light companion was talking about. The following essays are what I have figured out so far, through the use of my soul as my interpreter.

TELEPATHY

CHAPTER 13

Concord With Yourself

Concord with yourself starts with acceptance of what God made in you. The DNA as specific as your component parts, and those things you do best. Those things you love to do most. Like the state of mind that makes you the happiest. That state of grace that permits you the tranquility to have your own sanctuary. This state of mind is achieved by having self respect for the purity of mind that comes from never, lying, cheating, or stealing. The honest appraisal of reality without the exaggerations of ego, competition, greed, or lust Or, any other of the pretensions of the civilized world.

The requirement to achieve this end is to realize that in you exists three separate brain personalities that are virtually unaware of each other, and doubt the others exist. These components are the left brain, the right brain and the instincts. The left is deductive, the right emotional expansive, and the master brain the intuitive instincts. In the unenlightened the triune mind is dominated by the left brain, the emotions are suppressed and the instincts are repressed, out of the consciousness which is then dominated by the deductive left brain. These group oriented people tend to be logical and unemotional and insensitive to the more refined aspects of existence found in a less linear reality. This mental orientation is the birth place of the ego, and the competition males respond to in life. This is not Concord. This creates discord. The other alternative chosen by conformists is the suppressed emotional route, (the civilized female) This thinking largely is concerned with obvious sentimental attachments on the superficial level, that bind the participants in a constantly dependent struggle of the peer pressure. Everyone uses each other, to get them to conform to their precepts of conformity. Which seem to be different for everyone. Neither of these well thought out systems seem to work.

The third approach however, does seem to have God like merit. That is to rely on your instinct and your native primoral perceptions and allow your right brain and left brain to come down, off their mutual ego trips and allow the instinctive intuitions to take over using the right brain and the left brain as preceptors for the instinctive brain, (or that part of you being that is commonly referred to as the soul.)

When you allow your soul to take command of the body and discharge the memories of the left brain and the pent up emotions of the right, you achieve a state of mind that allows you to utilize the best possibilities available to you through the use of your multi-dimensional imagination, which is the key to your insight into God and the alignment mentally with God's initial indicator for the universe, "Let there be light". When you transcend this barrier of the left or right brain orientation, it becomes clear that your real purpose is the service of this expanding universe and you become a thermonoid - someone who responds to light - rather, than a humanoid who only responds to humanity. The purpose of your existence becomes changed as there is no longer any conflict for dominance between the three forms of consciousness. They work in Concord together. ...With each doing its own part, without the use of the ego, competition, and the worship of warlike Gods that come from masculine insecurity. Having Concord within yourself enables you to have Concord with those things outside yourself.

MULTIDIMENSIONAL PERCEPTION

CHAPTER 14

Concord With God

After achieving Concord with yourself, the next step is to achieve Concord with God. This is not all that difficult ...as there is only to realize that, "All the stars are in concert with each other, as man should be in concert with God". God's, purpose in creating light, and therefore inadvertently creating it's counterpart the black hole. And, God's purpose was that the conflict of these two opposite forces would give birth to all things that would help expand light while allowing those that wouldn't to recede from light and into a mutually proportioned black hole. You either live full throttle or you die.

Some parts of you can live while other parts die. Everything you say "no" to makes you smaller. Everything you say "yes" to makes you larger. Responding to the lighting potentials of God's universe is God's demanded prayer. You are part of God's universe. Even though man's attitude toward God is that God is part of man's universe. This of course is the ego of man trying to place himself at the center of the universe instead of God. If, man could fathom his minuteness in comparison to God, he would be able to comprehend the vastness of time. But, he doesn't and he won't. So, let's move on to the next appropriate dimension. Which is the Sun - the Sun is the child of the galaxy and is the daughter of expanding light and her father the black hole.

She generates her radiation onto her planet eggs in her solar nest in the form of solar rain in hopes of igniting them into a Sun'. The Sun, whose daughter, the Earth and her companion, the Moon are unusual only in as much as, through this Sun birthing process that may take billions of years, the creatures of the planet have been put through a process of predatorial domination and natural selection to see which species could control the foliage and other protective layers of Earth from the direct rays of the Sun which would cause turmoil and agitate the planet to super heat as part of the birthing process.

These things are inevitable but, are millions of years away. The period of time when this planet will be suitable for life as we know it, is largely dependent on the barriers of isolation we have between the organic functions of this planet and the rays from the Sun. This too is part of what God is - as God is all things having to do with light and as you have to do with light, so are you as God would have you be in designs of light. God is everything in the Universe that is made of light and black holes, and the darkness (nothingness) they are suspended in. We could say that God is the creator of light and the seeker of the satisfaction one gets from creating something that is usually expressed by "AH"! Having Concord with God, then, means Concord with yourself and Concord with the

Universe, and making your expanding light your prayer for your life and the dedication of your soul to God's purpose in this expanding universe.

God is, always, always.

CONTENDED

CHAPTER 15

Concord With Others

Having Concord with yourself and having Concord with God allows for a peace of mind that transcends the fear others conjure up in you with their discordant ways. Even though it is still true that negative people bring you down. If, you can have Concord with them until they can have Concord with you, this would be good. But, I personally avoid the sentimental attitudes that would nail your coat to that precept. That's what has worked for me. Keep an open mind until their agenda becomes clear. Your friends will never fail you, and your enemy's will be exposed in time. If, you're pure ...demand purity from them.

Water seeks its own level. You are as good as those you'll put up with. Choose wisely, your future depends on it. Don't be so sentimental you allow your demented relations guide your wisdom. Instead of, accepting everyone at face value until they rip you off, it would be wiser to only put up with people who think you're special and respect you and your friendship. Avoid people who "need" your help - But, help everybody you meet. See the good in everyone, but, expect the worst. Never listen to what anybody says, but, watch carefully what they "do". Don't favor one over another as only your close friends can steal anything of value from you. There are more people who are worth little than there are people who are worth something. So choose wisely who you would associate with or align yourself to. The real interesting thing about human design is that it's made to operate completely independently, if necessary. One must therefore deduce that this is the way God made man 'as an independent entity'. Not, the interdependent ball of conflicted conclusions he has become in his conformity to the peer pressure of the status quo of his civilized ways. His intuitive instincts are always there to save him in case he finds himself in trouble from following the unrealistic civilized approaches to solving the problems of nature. Man needs only to realize that nature is not a problem to man. But, that man is the problem of nature. Civilized man is out of sync with nature, and with his conformity to the 'civilized attitudes' of... "Let somebody else "do" if. Mankind has written his ticket to oblivion. And he's still too dumb to know. It's time we stopped talking about getting along with each other, (the answer is simple, "have Concord" between you) what we should really concern ourselves with is having Concord with Nature. Then we can be ourselves.

CAT PEOPLE VS. DOG PEOPLE

CHAPTER 16

Concord With Nature

Having Concord with other people is easy. All you need do is find a purpose for them in your life, and pay well. This usually will lead to a concordant relationship of a mutual prosperity. But, with nature it is a different thing. Man must realize that nature is perfect already and it is also a constantly growing thing. Unfortunately, man can only see from the perspective of his own needs.

And only his specific needs without regard for others. This will not do. What profit to stockholders if the oil spill destroys a coral reef? What good comes from feeding people if the disproportionate drain on the eco system causes the breakdown of the system on the intermesh of life? To save a few you must sacrifice everyone. This seems like backward thinking to the reality that God suggested when she said let there be light. All the other species and plants, bugs, birds, etc., live in light and in Concord with nature. Only man is the big Jerk who is, trying to destroy everything for everyone with his immature and childish ways. The needs of his disproportionate civilization are making the demands that will deplete the ocean of fish, the rivers of drinking water and the immensity of his wastefulness will destroy everything else. There's no Concord there! Concord is how you can use love in a positive way, as man has been known to love war, love hate, love lust, love lies, love corruption. All this would be eliminated when love is qualified by Concord. Concord becomes the use of love. Its direction, its purpose, by observing life through the eyes of Concord you can see everything that is wrong with the world and exactly what to do to correct it at the same time. The form of your observation becomes your solution - nature could be brought back to life by giving Concord to it with the help of love. Otherwise, bend over and kiss your ass goodbye.

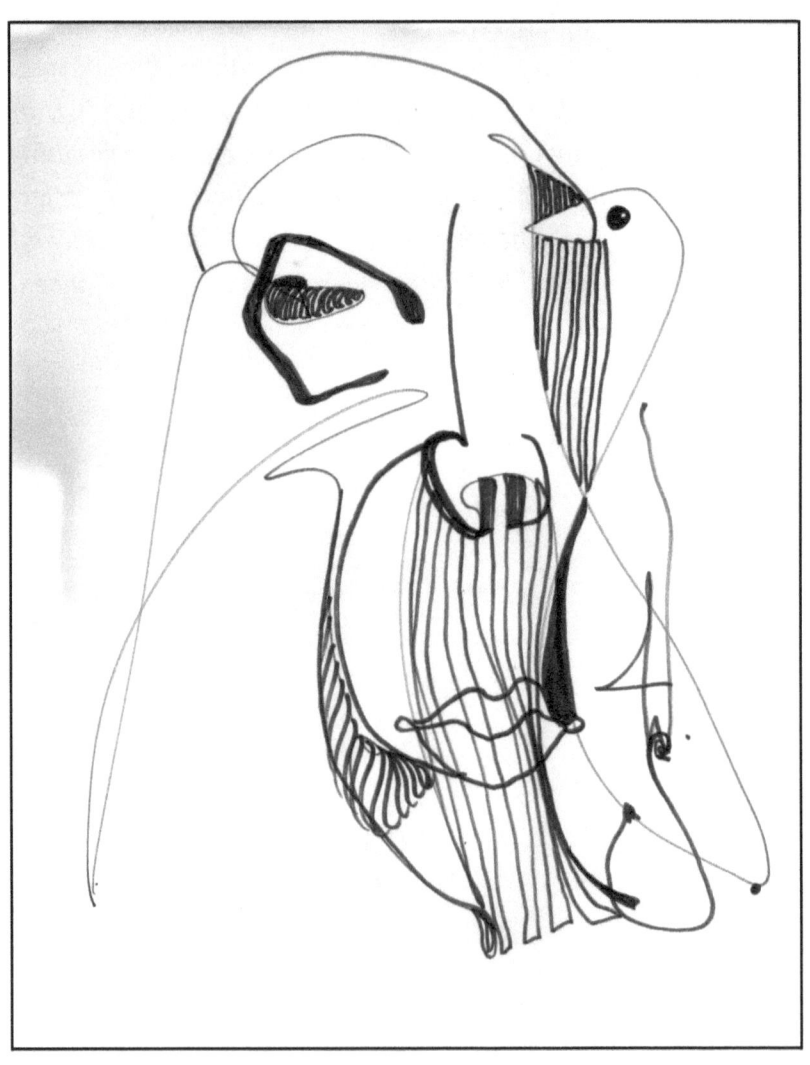

LANDSCAPE ARTIST

CHAPTER 17

Concord With Love

Love is a four letter word and can mean hell on many occasions. Man has a tendency to love anything he can concentrate on and this is usually his only focus. But, sensual dreams and frustration release caused the population explosion.

It's a man's inability to control and direct his sexual energy toward something other than his initial purpose of reproduction. This is all well and good, but, we find ourselves, now in a quandary. We either keep our frivolous ways or grow to a level of appreciation of our sensual energy. When we use it as an 'intensity focus' on something other than sex – say in art, or dance, or music where the person diverts their sexual energy into perfecting a personal dream, by putting reproductions of offspring on the back burner of priorities, while they concentrate their full energy to perfect the dream they have for themselves. They take the risk of dedicating "all" their effort to one dream and risk the casting of a game of pitch and toss.

All or nothing with them. Either win or be shot down in a blaze of glory. To be or not to be! The lust for life. The dreamer creating a life into an otherwise boring reality. This is what love is really all about. Reproduction is just the superficial part. The underlying motive is to create a universe of light. Love is light and light is love. And can be found in anything that is expanding in the universe.

You can have love with anyone you have Concord with but, you waste your time unless you wait for your soul mate. But, that's too simple for most folks and they spend their 20's and 30's in moral dilemma while they experiment trying to find the best piece of ass. ...All that heartache, expense, and delusion. ...All chasing down dreams ...that will never work. And if they had but, shut up and made the deal they would have been having fun until the real thing came along. When that happens, you'll know. Your body won't let you miss that one. And the best thing is that it's mutually reciprocal. Just, wait and see!

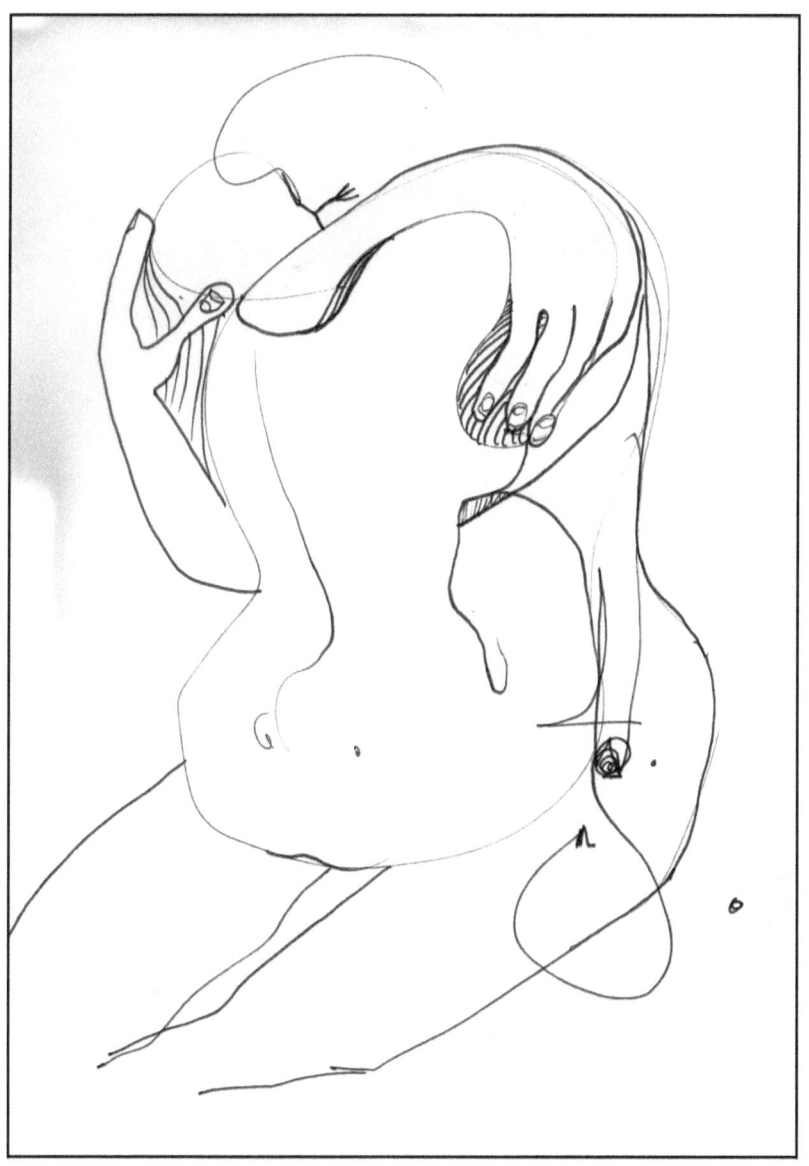

EMBRACE

CHAPTER 18

Concord With Business

Concord in business has to do with your seeking perfection in your habitat, fashion, decor, transportation, relationships, manners, good taste, style, consideration, comprehension, marketing, sales, public relations, customer service. Business has more to do with the way you conduct it than the bottom line. The honor, quality, concern, and class of your product is a more important proportion in Concord that it would be in some other motivation for the direction of your life.

If, you were as concerned for others as they were concerned for you, you'd have the balance of Concord between you and you'd be able to help each other grow in business. This, puts you in a very vulnerable position, as you are going out without inhibition, "they" must also. Human nature of the conformist left brain oriented mind would be very tempted to cheat and destroy the whole thing. ...As the conservative mentality is based on corruption and distrust. Conservatives only know how to save money they don't know how to make money. The extravagant side of their natures is what makes money for the conservative. The thoughts that come to him in hunches, and intuitions, and those things the artists and the open minded have all the time everyday.

You can't argue with a conservative on this point until they get some experience. There usual book learning doesn't cover those things that happen in the reality of experiencing the real thing. But, as soon as they get that real experience that everybody must deal with they become something other than conservative. Conservative thinking is for the narrow minded, sexually inhibited, and unimaginative.

These are also the qualities that keep thinkers of that genre in their place. Business happens in Concord when everybody makes money and everybody is in Concord with everybody else. Rather than the corrupt, back biting, rip off's that color the business world today. The Concept of Concord replaces competitions as the most celebrated word of the day and replaces it with co-operation and teamwork.

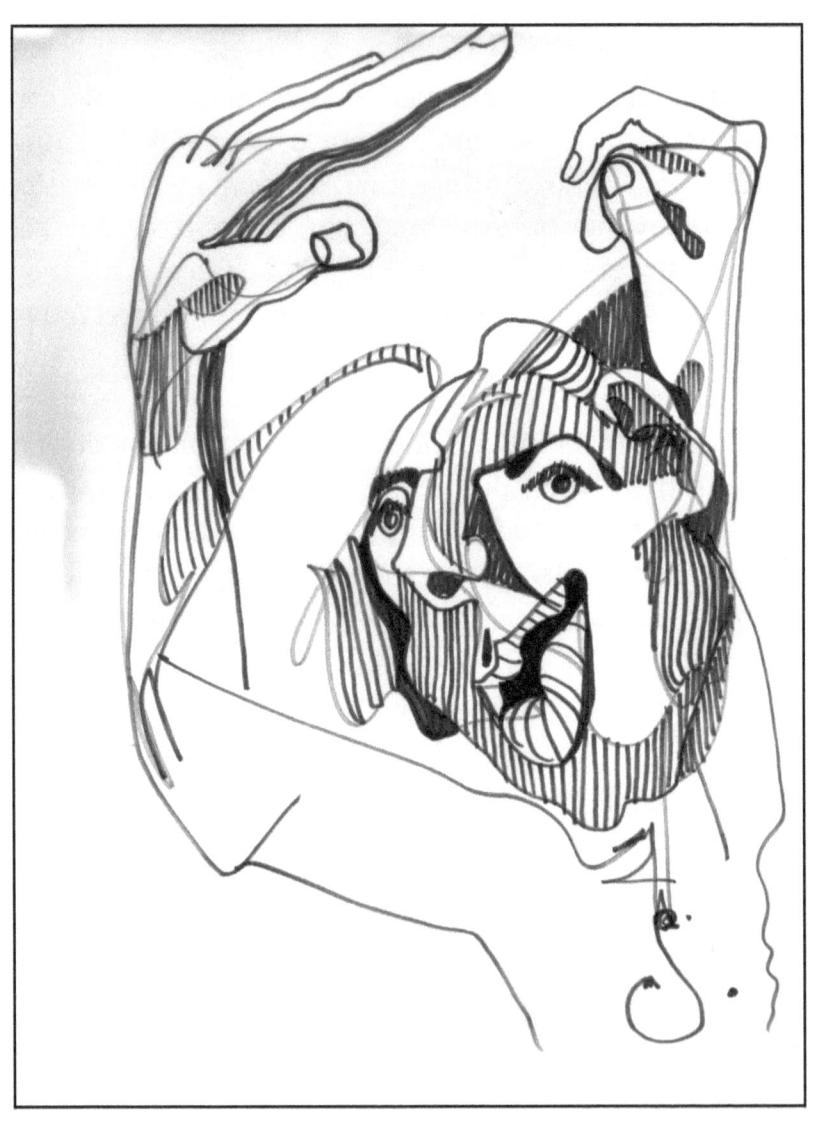

ENCORE, ENCORE

CHAPTER 19

Concord With Countries

There can be no Concord while the various ethniticities try to adapt to each other! Why should they anyway? Each has it's own uniqueness and produce goods indigenous of that country that have importability to other parts of the world without one or the other becoming destroyed by contact. With mutual respect Concord is possible; with mutual animosity only war and chaos can result. You can not complete your way to peace. Just as you can not compete until you love. Love is a good thing, with Concord in it! Without it, it won't work. Mankind is just getting out of high school, and he didn't learn anything in "his" four years, either. The world of countries needs the Concord of mutual respect that is required for the minimal contact. The germ of doubt and apprehension has been cemented in place after thousands of years of war and only a tactile peace. The apprehensions of man, dominates his thoughts, "not" his hopes and possibilities. My wonder is, how will Concord be accepted by; 1) the individual, then 2) his family, and 3) friends, and so on. Will it work at that level …Well it does in the stars… So, why not on this puny little planet?

THE SPY

CHAPTER 20

Concord With Religion

Religions and Concord see things in about the same way, but Concord incorporates their precepts into one concept. Then elaborates on the idea to make sense out of the whole package. The only type of religion that won't fit into Concord is war. And that is the black hole of man's existence.

The concept of a religious war is unknown to God - If God wants to destroy something, God destroys it, and God doesn't play around picking off a little bit at a time like man does. But, religion would have you believe differently - "they" say if you pay you'll get in good with the guys in charge, and they'll pin a note to your coat, when you die, saying to let you in for paying their salary. It's better than nothing in the war to keep man the monkey upright. He keeps slipping back to his killer ape status whenever he doesn't get his strokes.

Concord strives to bridge that gap and make the full circle in the patch work that is represented by all religions. If, you put them all together you'd get Concord. If, you brought them back to their inception you'd get Concord. Concord is what the universe is. It really doesn't take much of *a* religion to explain that. That concept alone explains it, defines it, and gives it direction. Everything else is just a stab in the dark. All is possible through Concord. This is not so with most religions. The beauty of Concord is that it can have Concord with all religions even if they "can't" with Concord. The reason being ...that Concord is what they are all after, but they don't have all the pieces and Concord does.

TOO MUCH CONFORMITY

THE CREATIVE AWAKENING

CHAPTER 21

Concord With Government

Government means control, Concord means flow. Government would have you live by a conglomerate of rules and directions of superfluous data. They would call this, "knowledge" and considerate it "power". The conservative agenda, of all politicians would keep them from having to make intelligent judgments on their own. The best way for an honest man to have Concord with government, Is to avoid it, at all costs. Government looks upon the honest as prey or they wouldn't lie to them so much. Concord and creative, "simple life", are a long way from civilization, and it's war like ways. Just as far as man is from his soul. The more time he spends convincing himself he's civilized the longer he must wait to have Concord with himself and thereby Concord with nature. And the farther he gets away from the perfect agenda for his life of skillful expression. Governments are designed by the warlike to control the meek during periods of "non-war". The military agenda controls when this in not the case. All in all government is just a justification for the popular to take advantage of the weak and unorganized. The mob controls the individual, instead of the individual controlling the mob. The dominance of the many over the few. With the vote of peer pressure determining the socially acceptable point of view and that way of thinking that leads to conformity and the automotonic way of life. Where a person's singularity is sacrificed for the benefit of the group. Life in the zoo of public opinion rather than a free and healthy over view of that abstraction we call life. It's good to get organized when you are raising a barn. But, not when you are creating a work of art, where the instincts are king and the vibes are your only sense of direction. A creative God, creates a creative child and a creative child emulates it's creative initial indicator. There isn't any room for deviant behavior in the neighborhood, of the web of life. There is but to do it.

THE SEDUCER

CHAPTER 22

Concord With the Practical Approach

The most practical type of conformity is the conformity to God and the concept of a light expanding universe. It is impractical to conform to the precepts of civilized man and his insistence on bending life's organic nature to fit his geometric plan. What is practical for civilization is distressing and non do able in nature. Mankind in general is still too immature to respond to this allegation as he is still too immature to realize his actions will destroy the world he needs to survive in. To have Concord with anything is no more than using a nurturing approach to your relationships and activities. This of course is the most practical thing to do. The other approaches lend themselves to selfish of peer pressure agenda, that can get way out of hand, when the vote is considered. And what the ignorant think is best for man... This is impractical.

The easiest and most practical approach to life is the one you are best at and have the least resistance in fulfilling. All else is a struggle as any stress free person will attest. A life that makes you happy is the one you'll like the best and is therefore the most practical to have Concord with.

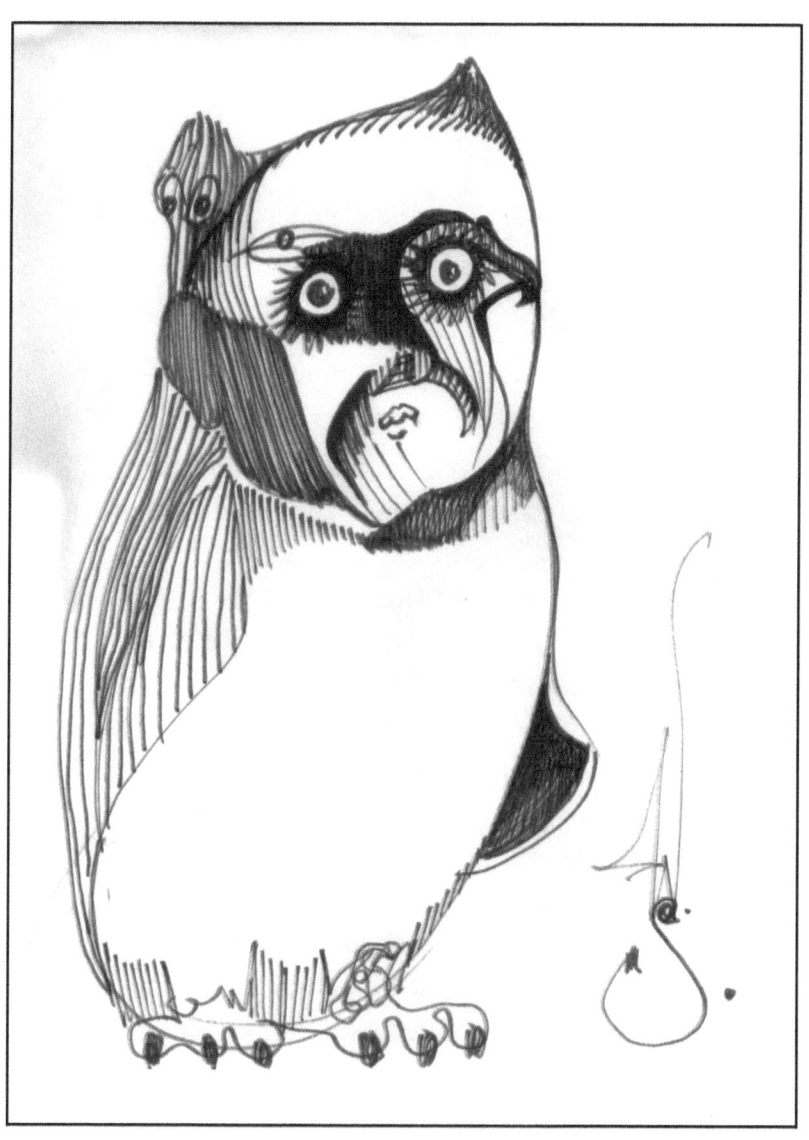

THE WISE OWL

CHAPTER 23

Concord With Generosity

The mind of the conservative agenda suggests that generosity is impractical and a foolish path to follow. The stress savings accounts and practical investment to develop personal security. But, what if you are not afraid of failure and you realize that generosity is where true success and abundance lie. Spreading the wealth that all may enjoy prosperity is the way that leads to even more abundance and the happiness and creativity that goes with it. God was not conservative when the universe was created. God was extravagant. God, went from nothing to the greatest expression of the universe in one felt swoop. That's generous, not conservative. You must be generous to have Concord, you must be generous to be God. You must be generous to have yourself, as you can only get to yourself when you give yourself to God - there is no other way.

Holding back for a rainy day only makes it rain everyday. The conservative holds back and the generous gives it away. Conservatives dry things up and generosity makes your cup runeth over. Extravagance always pays off in luxury. Conservation always ends up where there is not enough. Concord would be, when you are generous enough to contribute to the expanding universe with everything you've got. This is success and philanthropy at work in the world today. This is also what the Aquarian Age is all about and why we are moving in this way. God's children of Aquarius have returned to earth to set Concord in every way. What else do you have to do for the rest of your life?

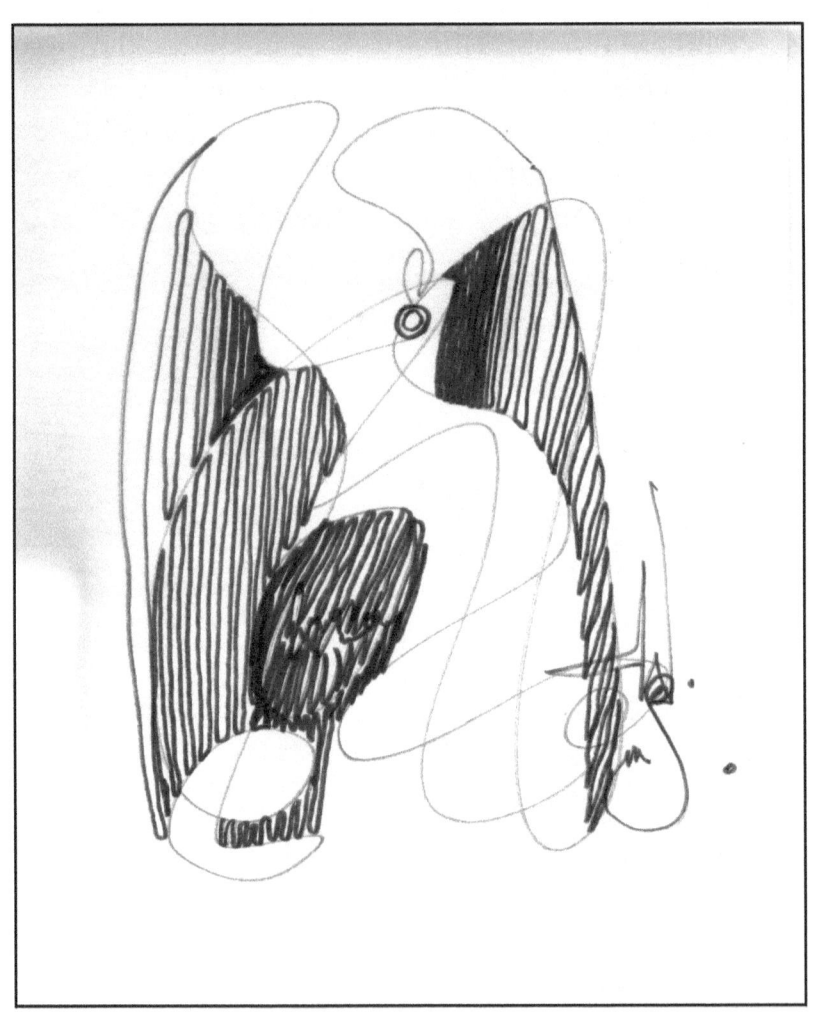

FEMININE ENERGY

CHAPTER 24

Concord With Concord

Being in Concord with Concord is the only way to have a "real" life. The concept of doing everything right comes to a realization in Concord. The striving for greater creative expression with every creative act is the way the Sun has Concord with herself. Having Concord with yourself, and the universe, and others is the way man has Concord with God and God's universe. The proposition boils down to how to have love with love in Concord. Seems like a pleasant enough sentence to me! God created the universe in a concordant design. Everything fits with everything else, but, in very different ways. So many so that the mind can never be stilled once ignited. Concord is a way of life, a system of healing, a character analysis, a plan, a direction, a telescopic sighting plan, an analog computer and an insight into life. All on just the surface of meditating on what Concord means. I now, realize, if only partially what they meant to, "Go back and do Concord." They meant go back and do a perfect life. Life without Concord is not worth living, love without Concord is unfulfilling …a world without Concord does not fit in a concordant universe. Concord is the purpose of life and having Concord with God is to live a perfect life. This is not theory. This "is" Concord.

This is all I've gotten so far on my understanding of what they meant by Concord. I know there's more to come.

DUCK OF DESTINY

PART III
BOOK OF VERSES

INTRODUCTION
TO THE BOOK OF VERSES...

The Book of Verses is a book of the contrasts found in civilization's library of thought provoking ideas that carry the weight of years and traditions of the history of man. We have come to this millennium change, which is the changing of the astrological age, from Pisces to the Aquarian Age of Concord.

BLINDED BY INNOCENCE

CHAPTER 25
God vs. Religion

Religion vs. God today because it says conform to society instead of the Godly way. The religious use the emotional bond to old and stagnant ways as grounds for their self righteousness and narrow minded ways. What God make true, was the other the flowering of every thing in every single way! There is no, stagnating hesitancy there. Just abundantly expanding in forever so many ways... God, creates with the Dower of the turmoil at the center of the Sun. This is what God would have you emulate instead church bound glum.

KASANDRA, DAUGHTER OF DREAMS

CHAPTER 26
Civilization vs. God

Civilization is when God got mad as she sent women and her mate outside the walls of heaven's gate. They were sent away, because till this day women and man think they have a better way in civilization than they do in God's natural solution.

All that is hurt and all that keeps him crying is wrought from his civilized striving. To fit and blend in, he sells his soul into sin, and can no longer see where he's going. Capture within his hesitant grin he lays there dying. His soul he repressed till the light in his chest only blinks once in awhile with knowing.

VULNERABLE TO CORPORATE AMERICA

CHAPTER 27

Civilization vs. Nature

Nature is the end of everything's trend from the smallest thing we can comprehend, to the largest thing we can imagine. In "the nature", that's free; the dimensions of three can be seen when you look for what can be round in nature. If you give up that knack for civilization track you'll be lost in the country and only know how to survive in civilization by remembering your job title. The real you will be lost unto you, as you are slowly replaced with your mask.

LION TAMER

CHAPTER 28

Man vs. Woman

Man verses woman. That's "true". It's man who is jealous of women. His competitive urge makes him disturbed when he thinks he's not winning. The women's a hero with her purpose in mind, to be the queen bee produce. When, mother earth created her for producing her spur, she let her give birth to man for protection. From his, "weight", he deduced he was superior to her roust and now he won't get any till he's back at his post as protector and ample provider.

THE SEED

CHAPTER 29
Conformity vs. the Creative

Conformity is only what you decide to remember about what other people would have you be, if they were accepted into their conformity. The thoughts that are used there are just the memories of what others think and adhere to. No thoughts of your own or thinking beyond your clones. That kind of thinking is left to the creative individuals.

THE MANY FACES OF SELF

CHAPTER 30

Numbers vs. Proportions

The numbers measure the size, dimensions, and the distance from here and the accounting of all the numbers. The proportions are felt; clean, fresh and in relationship to each other.... Another time, it's true, that the beauty of the proportions and disturbed by those measuring the numbers. Proving the details and for nerd, while the creative part is left for those who can feel the proportions.

WOMAN IS A GUITAR

CHAPTER 31

Chaos vs. Order

The randomness of chaos is the signals of life. The balance you find in them must come from within - the changes life puts you through will never end. The way your mind works in Concord will see you to the end. The disease of, "the out of order is often seen as something there to stop you rather than an indication you are going the wrong way. Chaos is the way things are, balance is how we handle it.

SHADOW OF INGRID

CHAPTER 32

Law vs. Justice

Laws are made by small minded men who can't feel right from wrong. Who because, of this they must write everything down. These laws of perceptual data begin to clog the mind. Where, to feel what is right or wrong has always been just fine.

Where, the laws of civilization, and that of modern man makes a mockery of the law. Anybody can get away with anything, as long as they play it right. But, justice would have everything done till everything was right.

THE PHILOSOPHER

CHAPTER 33

Conquest vs. Concord

Since the beginning of time, the masculine part of the Mother's creative machine has always been the one who sees the way that destruction can be right. This is a delusion they all must carry, so their ego's can be made to think they're, actually really right! It comes from the creative spirit of man but, it doesn't make it right In it's place, and at the right time, you may need to have it around. But, more often than not it's more if they're not around when you want to communicate or do something that isn't really boring.

THE WARS OF MAN

CHAPTER 34

Conformity to Man vs. Conformity to God

The conformity to man and his civilized ways is just a question of lasting for a few more days. The conformity to God and her expanding universe is the purpose of man but, man's got it reversed. He thinks that he who can juggle more than three i as smart as God, if not smarter. The frightening plea from the souls left at sea for their unknowing, withholding. It will tear your heart down from a smile to a frown, but, your conformity to God will keep you going.

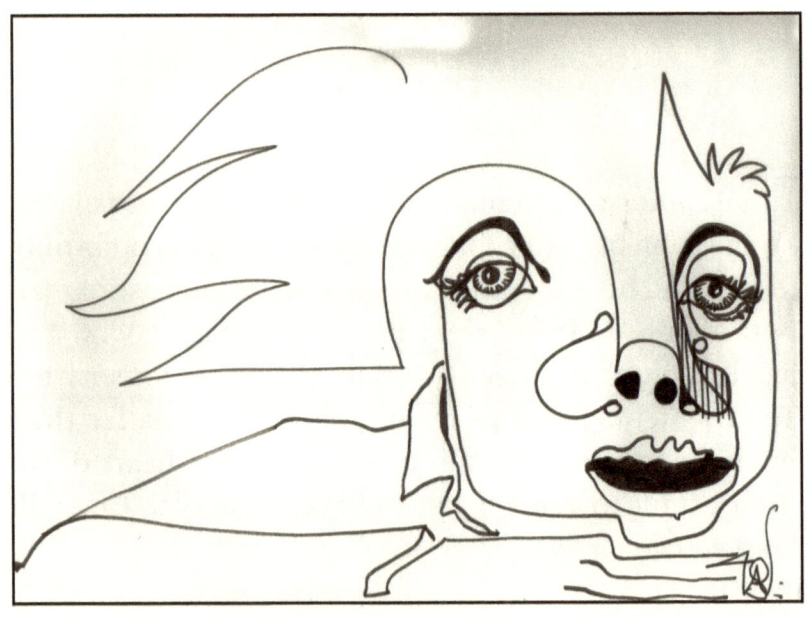

AFTER FIVE

CHAPTER 35

Conservative vs. Generous

The labeling and recording of things so we can keep score keep our profits from flowing out the but, increases our expenses by 900%. Just to know where some numbers say we are going. Having abundance to share is a better pack to bear and if, you give it away, they all owe you. The conservative approach where you count every roach is tedious and makes a poor showing. When you accept the over generous bid, you buy the luxury you would really have fun knowing.

AMUSED

CHAPTER 36

Confusion vs. Clearity

The start of a trip begins with laundry you need to wash to get going. The hindrance there is all in your head because, if, you weren't supposed to you wouldn't be going. The confusion from your doubt comes from unknowing shout of the unknown solution you have no time for knowing. The only things here are the echoes of fear from your own lack of knowing.

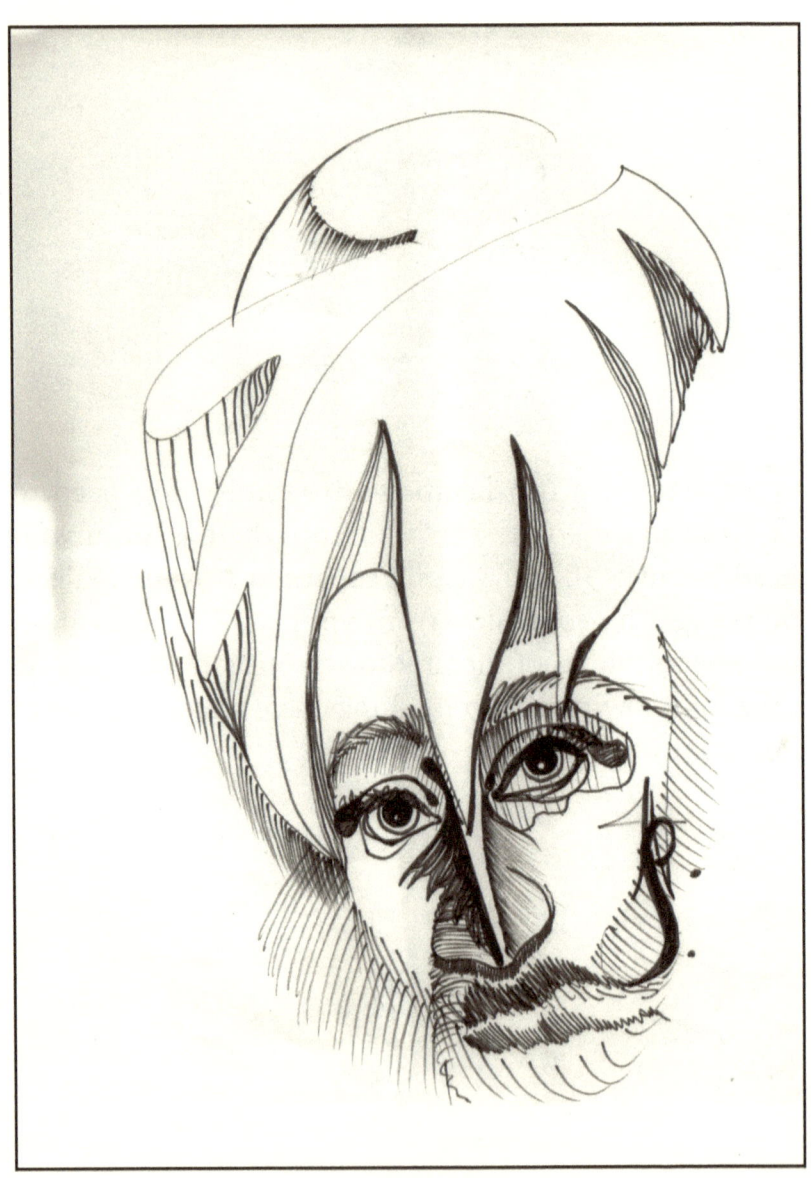

GYPSY

EPILOGUE

I hope you've enjoyed reading and viewing Will Stephen's vision. He truly was a messenger before his time.

Will and I were together for 20 years, until his death in 2001. We lived in northern California in a small town where his creativity could flow without the many distracting vibrations of a big city.

Will was intensely passionate about his work and getting these important, channeled messages out to the public.

This estate which I've inherited is now in my care. My intention is to fulfill his wishes to help assist in this transformation into the Aquarian Age.

This first book is one of a series of books that are intended to help to enlighten the individual and assist them to acquire their highest potential.

There is a website that is dedicated to Will. It contains his biography, and his varied unique art style, which so gracefully expresses his concept of "Multidimensional Realistic Expressionism".
http://www.concordfineart.com

Sincerely and with Love,
    Patricia A. Reeb.

BIOGRAPHY OF WILL STEPHEN

Will Stephen, An artist, poet, visionary, and philosopher. He grew up in Northern Wisconsin. His education was extensive, including "The Arts Students League" in New York City. He did various murals and commissioned portraits for several years of his career. He retired to Northern California to pursue his creative projects.